My State
WEST VIRGINIA

By Christina Earley

TABLE OF CONTENTS

A Crabtree Seedlings Book

Crabtree Publishing
crabtreebooks.com

School-to-Home Support for Caregivers and Teachers

This book helps children grow by letting them practice reading. Here are a few guiding questions to help the reader build his or her comprehension skills. Possible answers appear in red.

Before Reading:

- What do I know about West Virginia?
    - *I know that West Virginia is a state.*
    - *I know that West Virginia has mountains.*
- What do I want to learn about West Virginia?
    - *I want to learn which famous people were born in West Virginia.*
    - *I want to learn what the state flag looks like.*

During Reading:

- What have I learned so far?
    - *I have learned that Charleston is the state capital of West Virginia.*
    - *I have learned that New River is one of the oldest rivers in North America.*
- I wonder why...
    - *I wonder why the state flower is the rhododendron.*
    - *I wonder why there are so many historic buildings in Harpers Ferry.*

After Reading:

- What did I learn about West Virginia?
    - *I have learned that you can fish for walleye at Summersville Lake.*
    - *I have learned that the state bird is the northern cardinal.*
- Read the book again and look for the glossary words.
    - *I see the word **capital** on page 6, and the word **caverns** on page 13. The other glossary words are found on pages 22 and 23.*

WEST VIRGINIA

Hi! My name is Mateo. Welcome to West Virginia!

I live in Harpers Ferry. My town has many **historic** buildings.

The Potomac River and the Shenandoah River meet in Harpers Ferry.

West Virginia is in the **mid-Atlantic** United States. The **capital** is Charleston.

Fun Fact: Charleston is the largest city in West Virginia.

The state bird is the northern cardinal.

The rhododendron is the state flower.

We grow a lot of hay in West Virginia. It is used to feed farm animals.

Fun Fact: West Virginia grows around 894,000 tons (811,000 metric tons) of hay a year.

My state flag is white with a blue border. The state **coat of arms** is in the middle.

I like to explore Lost World **Caverns**. The caverns are 235 feet (72 m) below the ground.

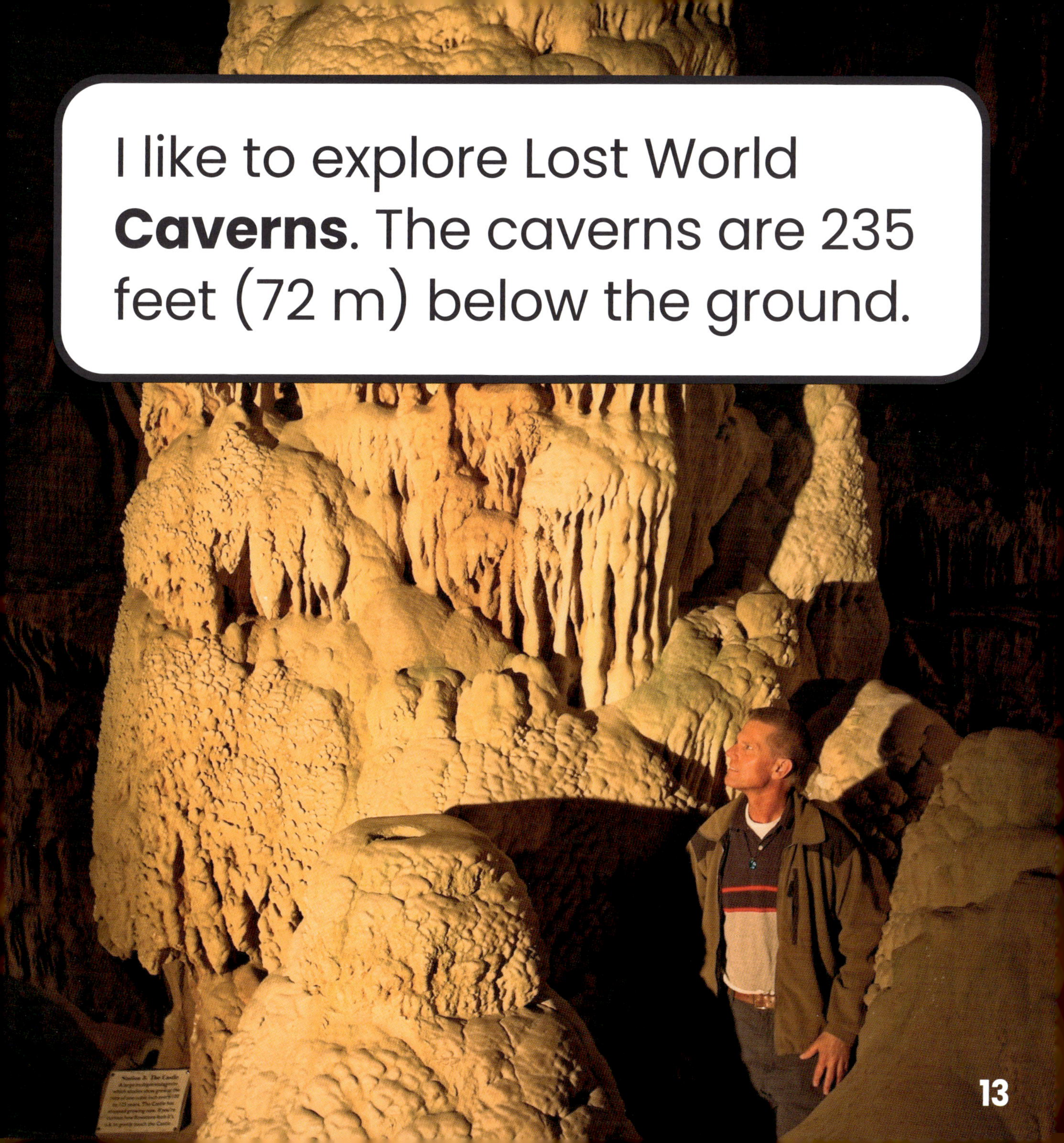

My family and I enjoy going to New River **Gorge** National Park. I like to see Sandstone Falls.

Fun Fact: New River is one of the oldest rivers in North America.

I like to hike at Spruce Knob.

Snowshoe Mountain has the best skiing.

TV personality Steve Harvey was born in West Virginia. Olympic champion gymnast Mary Lou Retton was also born in West Virginia.

Fun Fact: Shelley Moore Capito, the first woman from West Virginia to be elected to the U.S. Senate, was born in Glen Dale, West Virginia.

I like to fish
for walleye at
Summersville Lake.

I have fun learning about coal mining while taking a ride underground at the Beckley Exhibition Coal Mine.

Glossary

capital (cap-ih-tuhl): The city or town where the government of a country, state, or province is located

cavern (kav-ern): A large cave, usually underground

coat of arms (coht uv armz): A special group of pictures, usually shown on a shield

gorge (gorj): A narrow valley between hills or mountains

historic (hi-stor-ik): Something that is important in history

mid-Atlantic (mid-at-lan-tik): The northeastern area of the United States

Index

About the Author

Christina Earley lives in sunny South Florida with her husband and son. She enjoys traveling around the United States and learning about different historical places. Her hobbies include hiking, yoga, and baking.

Written by: Christina Earley
Designed and Illustrated by: Bobbie Houser
Series Development: James Earley
Proofreader: Melissa Boyce
Educational Consultant: Marie Lemke M.Ed.

Photographs:
Alamy: Oliver Gerhard: p. 13, 22; ZUMA Press, Inc.: p. 18 right; Hum Images: p. 19; Charles O. Cecil: p. 21
Shutterstock: Jon Bilous: cover, 4, 15-16, 23; Zack Frank: p. 3; Steven Frame: p. 5; Volina: p. 6, 22-23; Sean Pavone: p. 7; Bonnie Taylor Barry: p. 8; Anakumka: p. 9; Malachi Jacobs: p. 10-11; JoelMasson: p. 11; railway fx: p. 12, 22; Ami Parikh: p. 14-15, 23; digidreamgrafix: p. 17; Joe Seer: p. 18 left; Jim Vallee: p. 20

Crabtree Publishing

crabtreebooks.com 800-387-7650

Printed in the U.S.A./072023/CG20230214

Published in Canada
Crabtree Publishing
616 Welland Avenue
St. Catharines, Ontario
L2M 5V6

Published in the United States
Crabtree Publishing
347 Fifth Avenue
Suite 1402-145
New York, New York, 10016

Library and Archives Canada Cataloguing in Publication
Available at Library and Archives Canada

Library of Congress Cataloging-in-Publication Data
Available at the Library of Congress

Hardcover: 978-1-0398-0542-2
Paperback: 978-1-0398-0574-3
Ebook (pdf): 978-1-0398-0638-2
Epub: 978-1-0398-0606-1